Demons of Wrath

The Dark Fires of Attack Magick

Corwin Hargrove

All Rights Reserved. This book may not be copied, reproduced, in whole or in part, in any form or by any means electronic or mechanical, or by any method now known or hereafter invented, without written permission from Corwin Hargrove.

All images in this book are subject to copyright. Where traditional sources have been used, they have been crafted into entirely new images, and may not be copied or shared, commercially or gratis.

Disclaimer: The content of this book is based on personal experience and conjecture and should be regarded as speculative entertainment and not professional, medical or personal advice. The concepts and practices presented here are to be used at your own risk. Corwin Hargrove is not responsible for the experiences you obtain from working with the methods presented. It is hereby stated clearly and in full that the author neither suggests nor condones that you ever act in a way that can cause harm, and this book is provided with the understanding that the materials be used in accordance with the laws of your country or any country in which you are present.

Copyright © 2017 Corwin Hargrove

If you obtained a pirated copy of this book, you would be wise to discard it and pay for the real thing.

TABLE of CONTENTS

Demons of Wrath	5
Attack Magick	11
Preparation and Ritual	15
The Following Days	29
To Destroy Ambition	34
To Cause Anxiety	36
To Bring Depression	38
To Cause Regret	40
To Bring Exhaustion	42
To Create Conflict	44
To Ignite Aggression	46
To Cause Accidents	48
To Bring Bodily Sickness	50
To Weaken and Confuse	52
To Remove Control	54
Successful Attacks	57

Demons of Wrath

Demons, it is now widely known, can elevate people to great status, bring peace and calm, and do all manner of apparent good. Let us not forget that demons also excel when it comes to attack. This is a book of attack magick, using eleven demons of great power.

If you want to depress, weaken or harm another through magickal means, there is no better way than by calling on the fiery darkness of demonic energy.

This type of magick is, in my opinion, completely safe, and when performed as instructed, it is safer than letting your enemy continue their hateful work against you unabated.

If you have no enemies, you may still have a reason to attack another with magick, to gain an advantage in business or even in your social life. I believe that all magick helps magickal practitioners get in touch with who they are and confront their morals, and I believe that having the power to do harm makes you more likely to do good, for yourself and those you care about. And so I put this power in your hands. It was not always my intention to do so.

This book is quite short, dealing with only a small number of demons. There are eleven demons and their thirty-three servants. That is, each primary demon is called with three servants, and it is these *combinations* of demonic essences that create the power to attack. This is the secret you are paying for.

Everything you could want to know about demons is free online, except how to get results. The secret of results is often clouded. What I show you in this book are the secret combinations of demonic calls - using lesser-known demons - and the sigils that go with the demon names, to bring about powerful forms of attack.

These are the eleven primary demons and their powers:

Geradiel, to destroy ambition, bringing aimlessness.

Buriel, to cause anxiety, nightmares, and fear of madness.

Hydriel, to bring depression and weakness.

Pyrichiel, to cause agonizing regret.

Emoniel, to bring exhaustion and frustration.

Icosiel, to create conflict within a relationship.

Solviel, to ignite aggression.

Menadiel, to cause accidents.

Macariel, to bring bodily sickness.

Vriel, to weaken and confuse.

Bydiel, to remove control.

Of all these powers, the final one is the most cruelest and most potent. All we seek in life, when it comes down to it, is control. What else, after all, is magick for? What else do we strive to do except control our world? If you take away a sense of control, your victim is left feeling helpless, and helplessness leads to utter defeat.

Before going further, I must acknowledge the influence of The Gallery of Magick. I do not know them and have never met then (as far as I know, because they operate under pseudonyms), but although my magickal approach is quite different, I fully acknowledge that Damon Brand changed the face of modern occult publishing. He took the best lessons from the past half century, about how to reveal magick in a simple way, and he made a new format that everybody is trying to use. Including me.

If occultists have managed to make magick simple, then sharing it should be simple too, without fifteen chapters of obnoxious theory. And this acknowledgment comes because this book was inspired in some ways by a Gallery book.

I had been working on a book of attack magick for some time, but I got cold feet and could not see how it could be released without some degree of guilt. That is, I would feel guilty for potentially putting this magick in the hands of idiots.

When I read Gordon Winterfield's *Angels of Wrath*, I changed my mind, because I agree with the sentiment of that book. Magick performed without sincerity, in too casual a manner, will not do much harm. Whether you're stopping an enemy or trying to undermine a competitor, you have to *really* want it. If your blood boils, the demons will know. In that way, this book is actually harmless if used by over-enthusiastic kids and clowns.

Winterfield's book is a source of dark angelic magick, but I know many people prefer to use angels for good things and demons for bad things. Sounds simplistic? Yes, but it's meant to sound that way. You might feel a lot more comfortable roasting somebody with the fires of hell than asking an angel to give your enemy a dressing down.

There is much debate about what is a demon and what is an angel, and many conversations about the difference between angels and demons. Some say they are all neutral spirits, while others put them in categories of definite good and evil. You will even find some people who insist that the spirits found in this book are not demons at all, but angels of God. Given the fire and fury in their work, I think it is wise to consider them to be demons, but what that actually means may be irrelevant. The sensation and quality of the results are demonic by any definition of the word.

It is true that angels can also be wrathful, and it was when *Angels of Wrath* came about that I knew I should complete my work on demonic attack and release it to you. Originally called *Demonic Attack*, I have changed the title to *Demons of Wrath*, not to cash in on The Gallery of Magick, but to acknowledge their work and show that a demonic alternative is available to *Angels of Wrath* for those who seek it. My work gives dark powers of attack to those who want to work with demons. If you seek to use demonic attack magick, this is clearly a viable alternative to angelic power. It's one that can feel highly appropriate when you wish to attack.

With eleven different ways to attack those who displease you, there is no need for much more. You may wonder why the book doesn't go on for two hundred more pages and cover the seventy-two demons of *Goetia*. What you get here are eleven primary demons and thirty-three secondary demons from *Theurgia-Goetia*. All you need is here. I will eventually write my own book on the seventy-two demons and their skills and powers, but I am not a prolific writer, and that book is not coming any time soon. If you want pure attack, why complicate things? There is no need to go to other demons. Instead, use what you find in this book.

Attack magick should be used when needed, not as an experiment or to prove your power. If you announce that you are a great warrior occultist, and hope you can wield this magick to great effect, you might attract all sorts of unwanted attention. Take this warning seriously and use the magick only when you mean it.

If you want to work your magick well, do so in secret, quietly and without boasting. Even when your magick has put an enemy in the place they deserve to be, do not be boastful. It is risky to do so. Magick does not backfire or catch you out, but when you taint your magick with smug superiority, you risk making your subsequent magick weaker because of the subconscious effect of bragging.

The mindset of a smug person is not the same as the mindset of somebody who wields magick with authority and strength. When you succeed, relish your victory, but do not strut like a peacock. Be quiet and calm in your victory, and enjoy the benefit you actually sought from the victory, rather than the victory itself. If you sought a quieter life by silencing an enemy, then enjoy the quieter life, not the fact that your enemy has been harmed.

Magick is not purely a ritual that you do. It's woven into your life, and everything you do in relation to your magick affects the outcome of the magick. If you become a smug and obnoxious creep who proclaims to be powerful and evil, to frighten friends, enemies or whoever else, you only weaken your own magick.

As one of my mentors said to me, 'Shut the fuck up and do something else,' at which point I moved on and used magick to make some money instead of wallowing in glory. It was good advice.

Attack Magick

The demons in this book are from the second book of *The Lesser Key of Solomon*, known as *Ars Theurgia-Goetia*. Some of these demons were also described in my book *The Demons of Deception*, for deception is their most accessible power. They are also able to perform an attack, especially when you employ the 'wandering princes.'

The eleven demons featured in this book are known as the wandering princes or spirits, who can be called to accomplish great acts of wrath. I refer to them in this book as the Wandering Demon Princes.

The process described here works because you are also guided to call the appropriate servant demons that work with the Princes. By using these combinations, you can get excellent responses from the demons.

The ritual process is simple enough for you to get results without too much background information, and this book is therefore kept short and to the point, so you can work the magick if you see fit.

I will say clearly at the start that this magick does not work all the time, and if somebody tells you their magick works every time you'd be a fool to believe them. A wise occultist takes enough risks to allow some failure. That is how you learn and grow.

Nothing is infallible, so don't expect magick to be. Some bullets are duds. Machine guns jam. A perfect shot can be blown off course. The best weaponry in the world can leave the target unharmed. It's the same with magick. But having a magickal weapon – the magick of attack – is better than being defenseless.

Really good magick has a hit-rate of about eighty percent, if you've done personal research and contemplation regarding the issue at hand, learned the magick well, and know that what you're asking for is right for you at this time in your life. If your magick is not so earnest and well planned, then it works about half the time. If you don't pay attention and just throw a ritual together, it works about ten percent of the time. The magick in this book works more than half the time if performed adequately. You can make it work more than eighty percent of the time if you fill it with attention, commitment and with your rage. Rage is the energy of the magick, and it is a requirement if you want the best results.

If you can't generate that level of energy, then you don't really care about the result, and so it doesn't matter too much if it doesn't work. If *you* don't care, the demons have no raw power to work with. They need to thrive on your violent or hateful energy. If you do care, this is not an issue, and the energy will be present.

Even if you are using this strategically, say to undermine a competitor, the magick works better if you are filled with terrible hatred toward the person being targeted for the duration of the ritual. But only during the ritual. There's no need to become filled with hate in your real life, as that only rots you from the inside.

If you use this magick with full energy, against an enemy that you despise, it will work most of the time. If you use it strategically, to undermine and gain an advantage, it will work more than half the time, and perhaps even more if you put in the energy. It will not work every time. Get used to that idea now. You won't find a more honest occult book than this, but I've put the truth out there, and you can use this if you want. It's more reliable than nothing at all.

And seeing as I'm being honest, here are a few more things you should know. It doesn't always work instantly, and you may have to be patient to see a result. Often, you'll never see a result at all, because the victim hides it well enough to fool you. And finally, this magick is sometimes detectable by the victim and can be deflected by a serious occultist.

If you think that makes this magick crap, you've missed the fact that *most* attack magick can be defended against. Curses are easy to send, and protection is quite difficult to put in place, but *if* somebody puts up protection it is usually quite effective. The solution is to avoid fights with occultists. The other solution is to keep quiet when you attack, and ask the demon to let the attack take place very slowly so that the victim will not detect that an attack is underway. Even those who proclaim to do a daily banishing are certain to slip up at some point, and if your demon is working for over a month or more to slip through the gaps, then slip through the gaps it will.

Most people are *not* occultists and have *no* protection, and so the magick *devastates* them. One day, you may want to call the magick off, but instead, think ahead. When you plan the ritual, know the outcome you want and ask for it. That is what you will get if the magick works. Don't become weak at the knees after the fact. Put in some thought, do the magick, let it be.

Preparation and Ritual

Much of what follows in this section is similar (and in some places identical) to material from my book *Demons of Deception*, but please forgive the repetition. Revealing these powers is a major step. It is one I have not taken lightly, and this means that some essential techniques will need to be repeated. There are, however, many small variations, so if you have already read everything I've written, please do not rush through this text. It is quite different in places and requires specific modification for an attack to succeed. If you are new to my work or new to magick, work with what's here and you can get results.

This book is relatively short, because there is sufficient background material in other books (including my own), and the background material is not an important part of the quest for results. All I have attempted to do here is give you exactly what you need to make the magick work.

Not that long ago you used to be able to buy a book of curses or a book of black magick spells, and those texts never contained any theoretical background at all. That was in the day of mail-order occultism, when nobody relied on reviews and ratings. Now, books are overstuffed with theory to justify the magick. Not here.

In my other books, I've gone into *some* detail, but here, I'm going to give you a practical grimoire. I will not spend time justifying the magick, or convincing you that it is safe or worthwhile. You can make your own guess about that. You get what you need for the magick to work and whether you use it or not is up to you.

If you can, work your magick in the evening, or late at night, for the atmosphere of dark magick. An hour before you begin, dampen the noise; turn off phones, computers, the TV. Be alone, be quiet, and shut up and shut down.

Magick should be the focus of the time set out before you. A dark, quiet, calm and atmospheric house will get you in the right state of mind, but if you have to work in a noisy bedroom (with loud music used to give you privacy), it's better than sneaking and whispering. If whispering is your only option, it's better than nothing.

Get two candles; one black, one white. The white one is used to give some light in the darkened room, as well as signaling the beginning and end of the ritual. The black candle is for the ritual burning.

During the ritual, you write down your target's name on a small piece of paper, and your paper is burned in the black candle's flame. If you can't get a black candle, use a white candle. If you can't get a candle, use a lighter. If you can't burn things in your house, tear the paper up instead of burning. Every compromise *is* a compromise and makes the magick less intoxicating for you, but you can simplify the ritual down to nothing but the basic chants, words, and sigils, without any equipment at all. Do what you can and expect results that match your commitment.

Take every reasonable and sensible precaution to avoid an accident involving fire. If I say 'burn the paper,' make sure you don't get burnt, and don't drop it on the carpet, and secure your candle. Fire is dangerous, and you don't want to spoil an elegant curse by being too casual with flames. Be sober and of sound mind when you play with fire.

In each ritual, you burn a piece of paper. You write the name of your target on a circle of paper, so you will need to prepare these paper-circles in advance. Each ritual is repeated three times, so make three. Draw a circle that's roughly the size of an inverted coffee mug, and then cut it out. It's just a paper circle at this point, so don't be too precious.

Now write the full name of your target on the paper. When complete, it will look something like this:

If you don't know the target's full or true name, use what you know. I don't recommend writing, 'Jim from the house on the corner.' If you only know him as Jim, then write Jim. If you can find out his full name, do so. Anything is better than nothing, but if you are able to find out an accurate name that is currently used by that person (whether or not it's the one on their passport), it will work. If you only know a nickname, it can work, because *you* still know who you mean. If you have no name at all, it's unlikely to work in any way, so find something to work with.

The ritual works most effectively on those you have some connection to, even if it is only slight. A competitor may be somebody you've never met, but somebody you've encountered online, for example. But some interaction is better than working this on an utter stranger. Try using this against celebrities and you won't get very far. Its strongest effect comes when you know the person well.

The ritual is performed three times. If you hope for a fast result, perform it on three nights in a row. If you want a slow release of energy, and wish to ensure that the ritual gets through to the victim, perform it once every ten days, over the course of a month. Or, invent your own timing. There is no need to perform it more than three times, and doing so actually shows you sense the magick is weak, so keep it to a maximum of three. If you know the magick has worked as well as you want it to after one or two rituals, you do not need to continue.

Trust the magick, and it grows in strength over the coming days and weeks, so do not *look* for evidence that it has failed or succeeded. Simply expect that it will inevitably work.

For each demon, you are given a statement that will work. For example, with Buriel, you will see:

> "By the power of IAO, I call on you Buriel, Drusiel, Carmiel, and Nastros, to bring anxiety, nightmares and a broken mind to _____."

You replace _____ with the full name of your target. If you want to change the statement of intent slightly, you can do so. You may wish to say:

> "By the power of IAO, I call on you Buriel, Drusiel, Carmiel, and Nastros, to bring anxiety to _____ for three slow months."

Or you could say:

> "By the power of IAO, I call on you Buriel, Drusiel, Carmiel, and Nastros, to make _____ suffer from nightmares tonight."

What's already written in this book will work, but you can rewrite the statement to be more specific or exacting, and if you feel the need to specify a timeframe, then you can do so. Remember, it is up to you when and how you repeat the ritual. You may perform it three nights in a row, or once every few days, or every ten days. That is down to *your* feeling about the magick.

The call to IAO is a magickal call that gives you the authority of universal power, without actually calling to God. Some occultists believe that calling God to constrain the demons is offensive to the demons, but I have found this to be ludicrous. Demons will in fact whither when divine names are hurled their way. For these particular demons, however, I have found that using this lesser variant, IAO, which has been used in mixed magick of Greek and Hebrew origin, you are more likely to get obedient respect, and it's also easier to use if you don't like calling to any god. It's pronounced EE-AH-OH.

When you want to perform the ritual, have everything you need to hand. The small circle of paper with your target's name. A notebook, or sheet of paper, where you make notes for the ritual. Your candles and any holders they are to be placed in. This book. Something to light the candles with. Privacy.

Place the paper circle face-down on the table before the black candle, so that the name you've written is *not* seen by you. Light your white candle. (Turn all other lights off, if you can do so safely.) Light your black candle.

Scan your eyes over the uppermost seal in the demonic sigil. You can see that for each page, there is one large seal, and below this, three smaller seals. The large seal is the seal of the Wandering Demon Prince that you are calling – that is, the primary demon that guides the ritual. In this example, it is Buriel. Below this, there are three small sigils, representing three fiery servants that work for the demon; in this case, Drusiel, Carmiel, and Nastros. (The only exception to this rule is Geradiel, who has so many servants that it is deemed unnecessary to name nay or use any sigils for them, because they come so easily when you call to Geradiel.) Also, note that sometimes these lesser demon servants have the same name but a different sigil; Samiel, for example, appears twice, with the same name but two different sigils. This is of no concern.

Let your eyes take in the shape of the uppermost sigil. Just look at it, gazing gently, knowing that it's the symbol of the demon you are calling to. If you are working with Geradiel, you can now move to the next step, but if you are working with any other demon, now scan your eyes over the other three sigils. Know that you are looking and gazing at the seals of the demon servants who will bring potency and precision to this ritual. This process opens your mind to demonic contact.

Gaze at the flame of the black candle. As you gaze at the flame, chant the name of the Wandering Demon Prince that rules the ritual. In this case it would be Buriel, pronounced BOO-REE-YELL.

The pronunciation of the names is given in parenthesis. Say these sounds as though they are English and you'll get it right. BOO sounds like the word BOO when you jump out on somebody. REE sounds like REED without the D. YELL sound like YELL, obviously. Run it together, and you have BOOREEYELL. It's actually very easy. If you get it slightly wrong, it doesn't matter, because the demonic seals do most of the work. Do note, however, that G always sounds like the G in GET rather than the G in GEM.

Chant the name over and over while gazing at the flame, until you feel a slight change in the atmosphere. It might happen the moment you open your mouth, or it might take five minutes, but if you gaze at the candle flame and chant the name over and over, you will, at some point, feel a magickal change.

Do not expect a huge change. You might get a big effect – such as a rush of cool air, or heat in your skin, or a roaring in your ears. But it's more likely you'll get a mild shiver down the spine, or perhaps something even less dramatic, like the slightest feeling of the supernatural. If you feel *anything*, other than normal, that's a success.

If it doesn't work at all, and you sense no change whatsoever, the bad news is that it's wiser to stop and try again at another time, when your mind is clear of expectations, when you are relaxed, and when you are able to connect to magick.

It may take a few attempts. It usually works immediately. Expect success, and remember, the smallest shiver *is* success – it means contact has been made. Don't sit there thinking, 'I wonder if that slightly dizzy feeling I have is the demon, or if it would have happened anyway.' *Anything* that is different from normal *is* demonic contact. At this point, stop chanting, and know that contact *has* been made. (You do not need to chant the names of the three lesser demons, as they are named in your statement of intent.)

Now speak your statement of intent exactly as it is written (either in this book or as you have written it in your own notebook.). Say it out loud, three times. If you make small errors, don't worry, but try to get it right, and speak with confidence. Know you are speaking to the demons and that they can hear you. This sense of knowing is very important, and more important than how you say the names.

In this example, you would say, "By the power of IAO, I call on you Buriel, Drusiel, Carmiel, and Nastros, to bring anxiety, nightmares and a broken mind to Stephen Philip Johnson."

If you have a learned this statement, you can gaze at the black candle flame while you say it. If not, you can read it from your notes or from this book.

Again, scan your eyes over the sigil, gazing briefly at all four demonic seals.

Now take your circle of paper, and place it on your left palm, face up, so that you can see the name written there. You don't need to read the name, but it should be within your line of sight.

Allow your rage to grow. Whatever you feel about your enemy, feel it. If you do not actually have an enemy, only a competitor or other person you wish to undermine, *imagine* a rage against them as though it is real. This requires an act of will and imagination, and there is no shortcut.

Generating rage should not be any problem at all if you are cursing out of anger or a need for revenge. If this is more strategic, you can think about the loss you will suffer at the hands of your competitor. Let your rage and anger build. You do not need to direct it anywhere or focus anywhere. Just *feel* it.

When you feel like you've reached the maximum rage you can generate (and this may take two seconds or five minutes, depending on *you*), take the paper with either hand (or use an implement of your choice), and touch it to the black candle's flame. Know that as it burns, your request is being made real by the demon.

You may wish to light the paper and then place it in a metal bowl, or somewhere else, so that it can burn to ashes in a contained way. Or you may keep hold of it as I do, dropping the final fragment into the flame at the last moment – this can lead to you extinguishing the candle or burning yourself. It always leads to the ash falling all around the candle. If there are any unburned scraps of paper left, do not be concerned, but place them back into the flame until everything has turned to ash. If the candle is extinguished, relight it.

As soon as the last of the paper has turned to ash, scan your eyes over the four demonic seals in the sigil once more, and let the feelings of rage dissipate if they have not done so already.

If you still feel any rage, lessen it by knowing that your magick will work. Know that it has already worked and that the future you desire is coming toward you. This should take the anger away.

To complete the ritual, gaze at the black candle flame, and by way of thanks say the name of the Wandering Demon Prince three times, and the work is done. You only need to do this as an act of thanks.

There is no need to drum up the feeling of great gratitude. The demon has been called to work for you, and will.

Extinguish the black candle, then the white. (You may wish to turn the lights on before putting out the white candle., to avoid stumbling around in a dark and recently demon-filled room.)

You should now return to normal, and there's no better way to do that than to clear up. Make it feel like an ordinary mess that you are clearing away.

Forget about the ritual. The magick may begin to work immediately, or may build up its power over the coming days.

You will, of course, complete the exact same ritual (without varying the statement of intent), three times, either on three consecutive days, or on three days spread out at a period of your choosing, as discussed earlier.

If by any chance you feel lingering anger after the ritual, you should do, watch or read something that makes you laugh. It's unlikely you will need to, as the act of performing the ritual usually releases all the generated anger.

The ritual may sound complicated, but it is not, and if you read it carefully a few times, you will find that the process is simple. Once you are familiar with it, you can use the following summary.

To perform the ritual, you do this:

Prepare your paper circle, with the name of your target. Prepare your equipment.

Go to the place where you intend to work. Spend an hour settling down, away from ordinary distractions.

Light your white candle. Place the paper circle face-down on the table before the black candle, name unseen.

Turn off the lights if you can and light the black candle.

Gaze at the uppermost demonic seal. Then gaze over the other three seals below this one. Know these seals open you to demonic contact.

Gaze at the flame of the black candle. As you gaze at the flame, chant the name of the Wandering Demon Prince who rules the ritual until you feel a change in the atmosphere.

Speak your statement of intent (staring at the flame if you have learned it well, otherwise reading it.) Know you are speaking to the demons and say your statement three times.

Again, scan your eyes over the sigil, gazing briefly at all four demonic seals.

Place the paper circle on your left palm, so the name is visible.

Generate the required feelings of rage and anger.

When your rage peaks, burn the paper in the black candle flame and know that as it burns, your request is being made real by the demon.

When the paper becomes ash, scan your eyes over the four demonic seals in the sigil and let your rage go.

Gaze at the black candle flame, and by way of thanks, say the name of the Wandering Demon Prince three more times, and know the work is done.

Extinguish the black candle, then the white.

Return to normal.

The Following Days

If working the ritual three times seems like a lot of effort, ask yourself whether or not you want the result. Although you know that magick is not as predictable as a machine, you know it can work, and therefore if you want the result you should be willing to put in your side of the bargain without complaining about the effort.

Think about what magick achieves. It does things that would be impossible to do without magick, or things that would require extraordinary effort and risk. Three simple repetitions are worth your time and effort. It's true that generating the anger and releasing it can be emotionally exhausting, but the payoff is worthwhile.

When the magick works, if you get a good result, you may wonder how long it will last. The answer depends on many circumstances, the main one being the personality of the target. Send depression to some people and they will bounce back in two weeks, while others may remain that way for years, or even be changed forever. Being punched in the mouth only takes a second. You might walk away without concern, or you might develop PTSD. Everybody is different and everybody suffers in their own way.

In general, the magick resolves and fades out within a few weeks or months and has no more effect, but by then it can have completely changed the target's way of thinking and feeling. Be certain you want to make such fundamental changes to a person's life before you go ahead, as guilt is not an emotion you want to bring into your magickal world. If you do feel guilty, go buy an angel book and send blessings to your target, but to avoid this, know what you want *before* you use magick to obtain it.

Earlier in the book, I said you may not know whether or not the magick has worked. When you've purchased a book because you want revenge, and you want to see your enemy suffer, this can be disappointing, but I can't change the way the universe works, or how well people are able to hide their suffering.

It is undeniable that many people have the strength to continue *as though* unharmed when subject to the most intense curses. That does not mean they *are* unharmed. You may have been completely effective and achieved all you wish, and you will not necessarily know. There is little point in looking for the result, but there are many good reasons to assume that the magick has worked from the moment you complete the ritual.

It should be said, on a more positive note, that results can be obvious and almost instantaneous. Some people just crumble when cursed by demonic power, and you find out fast.

Occasionally, you will find out that illness or accident befell your target just hours or days *before* you carried out your ritual. It's well known in the occult world that magick always affects the past to structure the future, so do not be surprised if you find out that misfortune precedes the days of your rituals.

In many cases, you will see a very clear indication that it's worked, although it may take time. Even if you aim a ritual at somebody who is remote from you, you may hear from others (often much later) that there was a period of great suffering, illness, confusion or whatever else it was that you sought.

If you are near or around the person you are aiming to harm, you will probably see that they are struggling, but the important thing is not to hope for it or look for it. However, if your ritual has an intended knock-on effect, you *will* see that in action.

If, for example, you are confusing and weakening a co-worker, so that you can do better works and be promoted first, you will see your target struggle at work. This is one way that you can be certain that your magick has worked.

When forming the statement for your ritual, it is up to you whether or not you include such a knock-on effect. Some people feel a very strong desire to say something like, 'He will become weak so that he fails in his bid to be promoted.' I don't do that with these demons. I think it works best if kept as simple as it's written here, but you can change it if you want.

Letting go of your need for a result is important. Whatever need you feel, convert it to anger within the ritual, so that when the ritual is over you can stop caring about whether the ritual has worked or not. When you manage to let go this well, the powers are much more intense.

If you cannot let go and feel more hatred and anger than you can control, do not repeat the ritual, but you may want to consider sending a different ritual at the same target. If, however, you are actually suffering from that level of anguish, you are letting yourself be the victim. Use the magick to take control of your emotions, to release the anger and take the high ground where you are victorious because, in your eyes, that is where you deserve to be.

The Powers of Wrath

On the following pages, you will find descriptions of the powers that are available, with the accompanying name of the Wandering Demon Prince, the Three Demon Servants that work under that Demon (except in the case of Geradiel), and the suggested statement of intent.

The phonetic pronunciation for each demon name is given in parentheses. IAO, as mentioned earlier, is pronounced EE-AH-OH.

On the page following the call, you will find the required sigil for the ritual, containing four demonic seals. The sigil will be titled according to the Wandering Demon Prince that rules the ritual.

To Destroy Ambition

Call Geradiel to make somebody lose ambition or become aimless. You can use this power to undermine an individual's entire life by destroying ambition at a crucial time. It can also be directed at a target's specific project, if you only wish for your target to lose ambition regarding that project. If, for example, you know your greatest rival is about to complete a great work of art, you make sure they lose all ambition while you complete your great work of art.

The ritual does not work by causing confusion or distraction, but by creating a feeling of being aimless and completely lacking in desire, often with a dose of lethargy. Even the most determined people can be made to become ineffective.

The Wandering Demon Prince
Geradiel (GEH-RAH-DEE-YELL)

The Call
"By the power of IAO, I call on you Geradiel, to make _____ aimless, with all ambition replaced by lethargy."

Geradiel

To Cause Anxiety

Call Buriel to bring anxiety, nightmares, a general feeling of fear, or even the sense of insanity. Any emotion that contains an element of anxiety can be conjured through this demon.

Be wary of using this ritual against a target that you live with, because you have to live with the consequences of being around that anxiety.

It can be used as punishment but is also extremely useful in strategic situations, where you wish to make somebody else unable to perform at their best.

The Wandering Demon Prince
Buriel (BOO-REE-YELL)

The Three Demon Servants
Drusiel (DREW-SEE-YELL)
Carmiel (CAR-ME-YELL)
Nastros (NASS-TROSS)

The Call
"By the power of IAO, I call on you Buriel, Drusiel, Carmiel, and Nastros, to bring anxiety, nightmares and a broken mind to _____."

Buriel

To Bring Depression

Hydriel can be called to bring a feeling of depression, weakness or inability. You can bring a general sense of darkness and misery to the target's entire life, or you can call for weakness in specific areas of the target's life, such as work, projects or relationships. Fast results are possible, but slow results are more likely with this ritual.

The Wandering Demon Prince
Hydriel (HIGH-DREE-YELL)

The Three Demon Servants
Camiel (CAH-ME-YELL)
Arbiel (ARE-BEE-YELL)
Samiel (SAH-ME-YELL)

The Call

"By the power of IAO, I call on you Hydriel, Camiel, Arbiel, and Samiel, to bring a dark cloud of depression and weakness to _____."

Hydriel

To Cause Regret

Pyrichiel will cause your target to feel deep and agonizing regret. The wording of the call is kept very simple, and if left this way, it will cause a general and uncertain feeling of regret that can be baffling and painful for the victim. You can easily make it more specific by adding, "about the way he treated me," or anything else you wish. Being more specific can give you more personal satisfaction.

The Wandering Demon Prince
Pyrichiel (PIE-RICK-EE-YELL)

The Three Demon Servants
Nemariel (NEM-ARE-EE-YELL)
Damarsiel (DAMN-ARE-SEE-YELL)
Cardiel (CARD-EE-YELL)

The Call
"By the power of IAO, I call on you Pyrichiel, Nemariel, Damarsiel, and Cardiel, to cause _____ to feel intense regret."

Pyrichiel

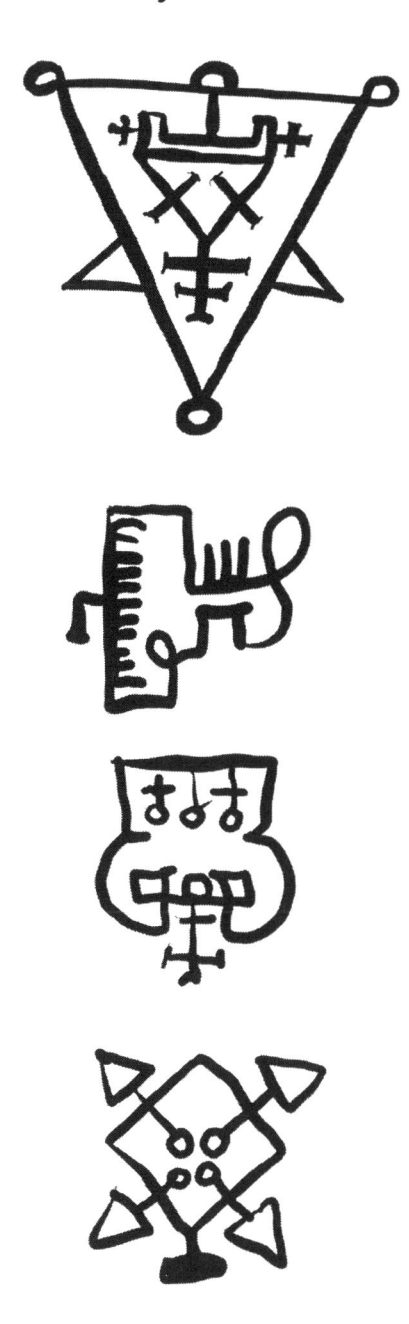

To Bring Exhaustion

Emoniel will bring exhaustion and frustration to your target. Although these may seem like quite different emotions, exhaustion is much more enervating when it is accompanied by frustration. The ritual won't attract more frustrating occurrences but will make things *appear* more frustrating. The sensation of exhaustion can be so overwhelming that your target will feel unwell, or even that an entire change of lifestyle is required. Like many of the rituals in this book it can be used as a punishment, or to make somebody weaker and more vulnerable to influence or more ordinary forms of competition.

The Wandering Demon Prince
Emoniel (EM-AWE-KNEE-YELL)

The Three Demon Servants
Carnodiel (CAR-NAW-DEE_YELL)
Ermeniel(URR-MEN-EE-YELL)
Panuel (PAH-NOO-ELL)

The Call
"By the power of IAO, I call on you Emoniel, Carnodiel, Ermeniel, and Panuel, to cause _____ to suffer from exhaustion and frustration."

Emoniel

To Create Conflict

Icosiel brings conflict to a relationship. The ritual can be used to encourage a romantic relationship to end, but to finish it off, you may have to step in and show that you are a calmer person than the one you're trying to replace. There are many other crafty uses for this ritual, but be careful about using it, because it can be strenuous to be near somebody who is conflicted. No ritual is designed to make people turn to violence, and the conflict is purely emotional. Don't expect targets to attack each other, but do expect enough conflict to damage a relationship, potentially beyond repair. Both targets are named in the call.

The Wandering Demon Prince
Icosiel (EE-CAW-SEE-YELL)

The Three Demon Servants
Larphiel (LAR-FEE-YELL)
Thanaliel (THAH-NAH-LEE-YELL)
Zosiel (ZAW-ZEE-YELL)

The Call
"By the power of IAO, I call on you Icosiel, Larphiel, Thanaliel and Zosiel, to bring fierce conflict between _____ and _____."

Icosiel

To Ignite Aggression

Solviel will make another person aggressive, so use this only if you know you can steer clear of that person. The intent of the ritual is to make the person aggressive to a boss, colleague, business partner, or random stranger, bringing destruction, loss of reputation or even arrest. Know that the ritual may cause collateral damage, and use only when you believe such aggression will lead to the target's downfall. Those who rely on high status are most susceptible to this ritual. Note that it does not lead to violence unless the person is intrinsically violent, but it reduces inhibitions so that the target becomes needlessly aggressive at inappropriate times.

The Wandering Demon Prince
Solviel (SOLVE-EE-YELL)

The Three Demon Servants
Prasiel (PRAH-SEE-YELL)
Caroel (CAR-AWE-YELL)
Penador (PEN-ADORE)

The Call
"By the power of IAO, I call on you Solviel, Prasiel, Caroel, and Penador, to ignite a fire of untamed aggression within _____."

Solviel

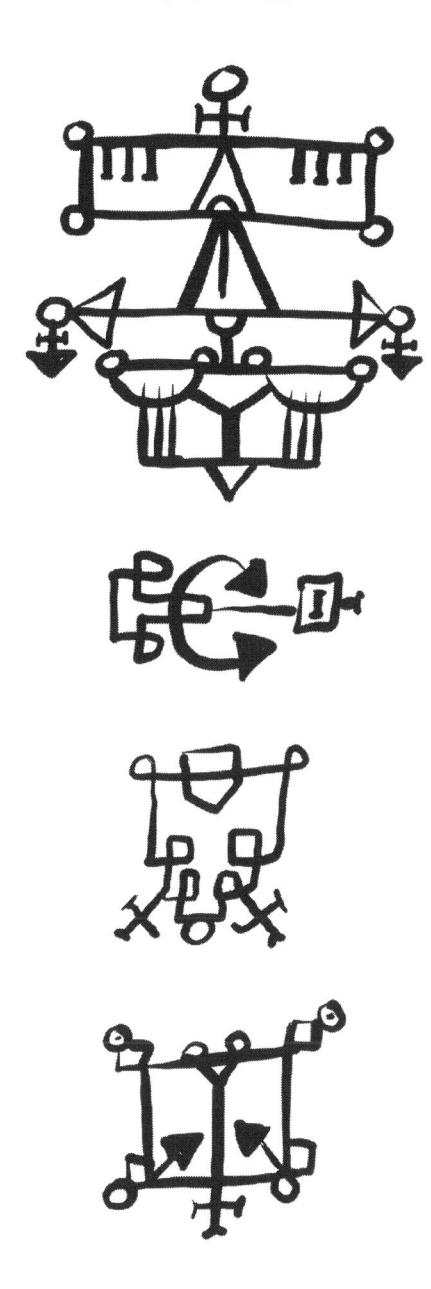

To Cause Accidents

Menadiel can bring a series of strange and frightening accidents to your target, without causing intense suffering. This is not a death curse but can lead to small accidents that involve cuts, and larger accidents such as falls. It brings general misfortune involving machinery, devices, vehicles and more abstract things such as finances, tax, and legal issues. It has the additional effect of making the target feel like they are the victim of eternal misfortune. This works best when it's not made overly specific, and the wording below is very effective.

The Wandering Demon Prince
Menadiel (MEN-AH-DEE-YELL)

The Three Demon Servants
**Benadiel (BEN-AH-DEE-YELL)
Charsiel (CAR-SEE-YELL)
Samiel (SAH-ME-YELL)**

The Call
"By the power of IAO, I call on you Menadiel, Benadiel, Charsiel, and Samiel, to bring accidents and misfortune to _____."

Menadiel

To Bring Bodily Sickness

Macariel can bring sickness to your target, with the emphasis being on bowel and gut problems. The ritual does not cause mental anguish beyond that which is caused by the physical discomfort. The sickness will usually evolve within a week, but if a time constraint is vital to your working, include it in the wording, but know that any such constraint reduces the likelihood of success.

The Wandering Demon Prince
Macariel (MAH-CAR-EE-YELL)

The Three Demon Servants
**Varpiel (VARP-EE-YELL)
Gremiel (GREM-EE-YELL)
Aromusiel (ARROW-MOO-SEE-YELL)**

The Call
"By the power of IAO, I call on you Macariel, Varpiel, Gremiel, and Aromusiel, to bring bodily sickness to _____."

Macariel

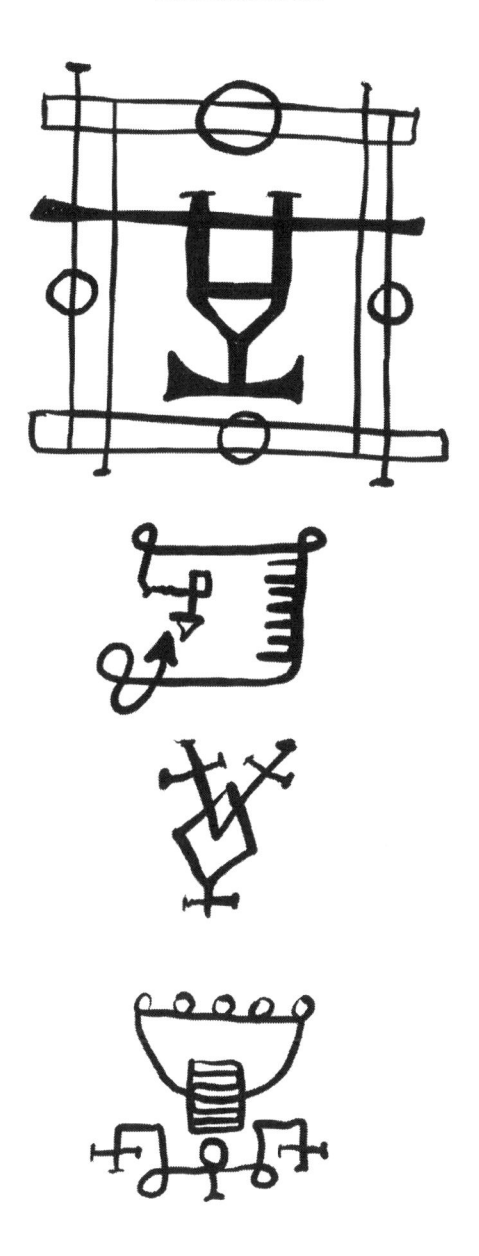

To Weaken and Confuse

Vriel will weaken and confuse your target. The weakness will always be quite general, but you can direct the confusion to a particular area of the target's life if that is important to you. The result of this ritual is that the person becomes ineffective, unable to make good decisions and also, as a side-effect, difficult for other people to like. The name Vriel is sometimes written is Uriel, like the angel, but you get the best effect using the Vriel pronunciation.

The Wandering Demon Prince
Vriel (VUH-REE-YELL)

The Three Demon Servants
Darpios (DAR-PEA-OZ)
Hermon (HAIR-MAWN)
Adrensis (AH-DREN-SEES)

The Call

"By the power of IAO, I call on you Vriel, Darpios, Hermon, and Adrensis, to weaken and confuse _____."

Vriel

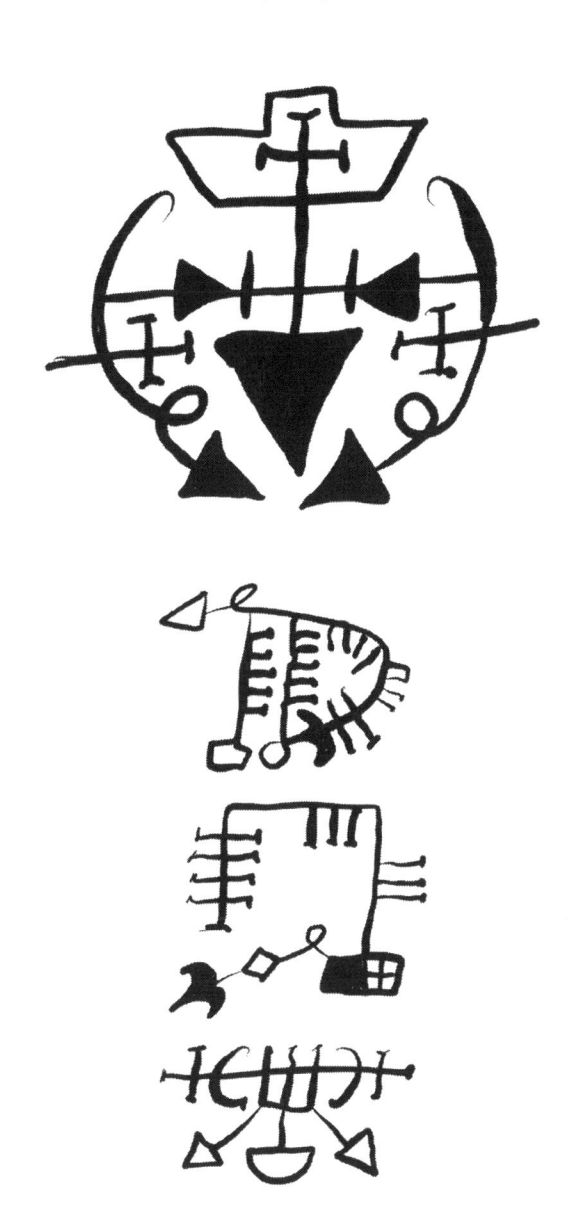

To Remove Control

Bydiel will bring a sense of hopelessness to your target by taking away their sense of control. We cope with life by feeling that we have control over our environment. When that is eroded, few people can maintain a sense of who they are. This ritual will make your target feel that all they do goes astray, even if that is not the case. They will learn to feel helpless, becoming weak and ineffective. Like all the magick in this book, it does not work every time, but when a result is evident, it can be terrible. Its effects may be seen in days, but for some people, the best results are brought about by the slow rotting of hope.

The Wandering Demon Prince
Bydiel (BYE-DEE-YELL)

The Three Demon Servants
Armoniel (ARE-MAW-KNEE-YELL)
Lemoniel (LEH-MAW-KNEE-YELL)
Mudriel (MOO-DREE-YELL)

The Call
"By the power of IAO, I call on you Bydiel, Armoniel, Lemoniel, and Mudriel, to remove control and hope from _____."

Bydiel

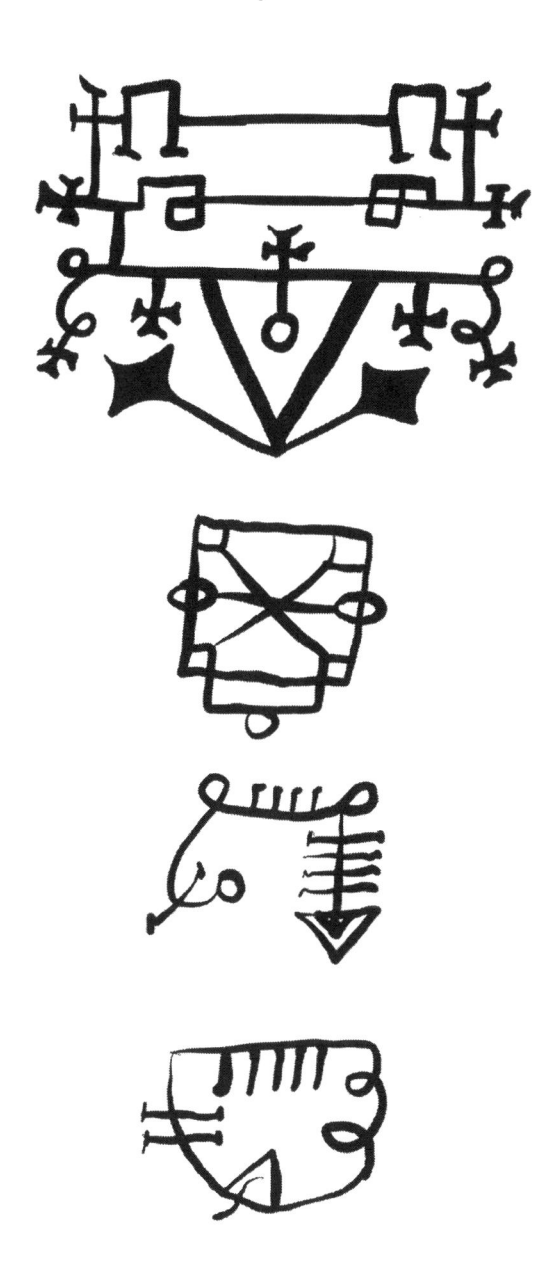

Successful Attacks

Is it dangerous to attack? Can you trust demons? Will the evil return to haunt you? These thoughts are certain to be on your mind.

When I have been in need of extreme defense or strategic advantage, demonic attack has worked for me. By silencing and making still those who would harm my loved ones and me, I brought more peace to the world than if I had tried to tame the situation with angelic power.

I don't deny the power of angels, but I do acknowledge the raw power of demons, and the balance they bring to a magickal life.

Whether you choose to use them or not is up to you, but know that any apparent side-effect or backlash comes from your own guilty imagination.

Do the work as though you mean it. Want the result in a genuine way. You have nothing to fear but success.

Sincerely,

Corwin Hargrove

Printed in Poland
by Amazon Fulfillment
Poland Sp. z o.o., Wrocław